The Promise Ring Crown

Tiffany Anita McClure

Copyright © 2021 by Tiffany Anita McClure

All rights reserved. No part of this publication may be reproduced, distributed or transmitted in any form or by any means, including photocopying, recording, or other electronic or mechanical methods, without the prior written permission of the publisher, except in the case of brief quotations embodied in critical reviews and certain other noncommercial uses permitted by copyright law. For permission requests, write to the publisher, addressed "Attention: Permissions Coordinator," at the address below.

Tiffany Anita McClure/Rejoice Essential Publishing

PO BOX 512

Effingham, SC 29541

www.republishing.org

Unless otherwise indicated, scripture is taken from the King James Version.'

The Promise Ring Crown/Tiffany Anita McClure

ISBN-13: 978-1-956775-12-9

May you walk in the fullness of God and stay in His presence until He returns on that glorious day. May God take you to a place where you can feel His love overflow.

~Tiffany Anita McClure

Dedication

I dedicate this book to God and thank Him for all that He has done in my life. I am grateful to Him for placing it in my heart to tell my story. I hope you are blessed by it!

TABLE OF CONTENTS

Introduction..1
CHAPTER 1: The Beginning............................2
CHAPTER 2: The Start Of My Ministry.........5
CHAPTER 3: Answering the Call....................7
CHAPTER 4: Spiritual Warfare......................13
CHAPTER 5: The Lord's Desire....................17
CHAPTER 6: Go Deeper in Christ................23
CHAPTER 7: A Promised Crown..................25
CHAPTER 8: An Heir of God........................27
Prayer Of Salvation.......................................29
About The Author..31

Introduction

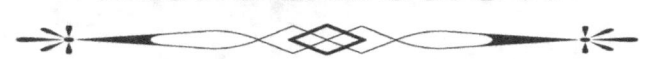

I felt led to share my testimony in this book after seeing how much God has done for me in my life after answering my calling, and allowing the Holy Spirit to lead. I hope this book inspires you to go deeper in your walk with the Lord. I pray it encourages you to never give up on God no matter what. God is pleased when you continually seek Him. Always be available when the Lord calls on you. You are producing a great reward in heaven. God bless you all!

ONE

The Beginning

I grew up in a Christian home where we went to church 3 times a week. I got saved at a young age about the age of 8 years old because I knew when I died that I wanted to go to heaven and be with the Lord. When I got to college I backslid and I began to drink a lot, and I was really blinded by some of the relationships that I was in at the time that I thought were good for me. I know that my parents had been praying for me the entire time I was in college because there was a hedge of protection around me! As a child I remember seeing my parents praying and doing devotionals all the time. I would see them praying all the time anywhere just on their knees reverencing the Lord.

The Beginning

After graduating from college and meeting the one who is now my husband, I rededicated my life to Christ and really started getting in God's word. The word literally transformed my life. As I stayed in God's word I began to find out who He is, and who I am. With all that sin that I had been doing Jesus took me back. I learned that Jesus chose me, and had great plans for me to use me for His glory even when I felt like I wasn't good enough and didn't measure up. He saw me as a vessel fit for use.

Even though I knew that God was going to use me for His glory after I rededicated my life to Him, I always kind of felt like I didn't measure up, or that I wasn't living up to all that God, or anyone else wanted me to be. I felt ordinary. And I would wonder why God wasn't using me in a particular way that I wanted to be used in. I would question God and ask, "Why can't I move people and get them into your presence in the particular area that I had been praying about?" God showed me that the area that I was seeking wasn't the area where He designed for me to be. As I continued to pray and hearkened to the voice of God He showed me where He wanted me to go and I could see Him work and move like never before. It was amazing!

Then the Lord revealed to me people who have talents and are moving people, but their hearts are far from God. He started revealing to me the hearts and spirits of certain pastors, speakers and people around me. The Lord showed me that He doesn't care how talented or gifted a person is if they aren't doing it for Him. If His spirit isn't there it is pointless. And I was like wow! Thank you for that discernment, Lord.

To see the miracles that took place in my life and how the Lord was there with me in my college years and through some things that I've gone through recently is just incredible. I am now able to look back on everything, and see that where the Lord has me today was all part of His plan for me the entire time. To use me for His glory! Then the Lord really started moving in my life, and what I am about to tell you next is when the Lord really called me to be used and began a great work in me.

TWO

The Start Of My Ministry

The Lord led me to read the bible in one year and share it on YouTube for others who wanted to get involved in Dec of 2019. I was apprehensive at first because I am kind of a private person when it comes to sharing personal videos, but I listened to His voice. A few months after I started reading it the coronavirus pandemic hit which confirmed and reassured me why I was led to go on YouTube. There were so many people who could not go to church that turned to YouTube to listen to the word. This was a time when we all needed to reflect and claim God's powerful promises found in scripture no matter what the media was feeding us. God had called me to be a light during this devastating time through feeding others His word. I was so amazed to see how God spoke during this time. It blessed me to step out on faith and really see how people were growing in Christ by hearing the word! Shortly after finishing the bible in one year I began praying healing prayers for many for a period of 6 months, and I felt God's gift of healing start to manifest and quicken in me. The Lord had also started giving me dreams about things that He was revealing to me and wanted me to do.

THREE

Answering The Call

One day the Lord spoke to my spirit and said "I have given you the ability to heal, I need you to go out in the community and lay hands on people and pray over them." I thought to myself "Where am I gonna go? Show me what you want me to do if this is what I'm supposed to be doing?" I didn't know if God wanted me to go to the assisted living homes, to the jails or what... and I was calling around to these different places. I thought, how am I supposed to do this in this pandemic? This needs to be put on hold. So I said, "Ok I'm gonna pray about this situation." As many of you know when you ask and pray, God answers!

I came across a minister's channel and saw that he was doing street ministry with a team in my area where they go out and spread the gospel of Christ. I said to myself "look at God." I prayed and asked God to confirm if the ministry that He led me to was in fact where He wanted me to be. When I got confirmation I began to go out on the streets telling people about the good news of Jesus Christ. I went out street preaching one time, and I saw the need that was there to bring lost souls to Christ and never stopped going back since. I'm telling you, it's amazing how God orchestrates things so perfectly for His chosen. All He is asking for is our yes. **For many are called, but few are chosen. — Matthew 22:14 KJV.** I have seen the power of God out there, and have experienced the amazing testimonies of so many that we have prayed over. We have to walk and live in that power and authority!

We prayed for an individual who had a series of health problems, and a brain tumor. He had been taking medication for years and decided to step out on faith, trust God and receive the healing prayers we prayed over him. He has not

only been medication free, but pain free for almost a month now. Glory to God!

We had been praying for someone who needed their social security card and ID card to get a job. The manager of a corporation took this young guy in from off the streets, and allowed him to work while he was waiting to get his social security card and ID. This is the power of prayer!

One day in particular we came across a woman standing on the corner who looked as if she was waiting for the street ministry team. She had many bandages all over her legs. On each bandage there was a lie written about who she thought she was. She told us about how she hurt God so much, and how she had done things that she regretted that she thought the Lord would hate her for. We began to reveal to her the love of God, and told her that she was none of those things that she had stuck on herself. When we laid hands on her and began to pray for her deliverance, we literally heard the demonic entities come out of her. I had not experienced anything like it. When we walk and live in the power and authority that we have in Jesus name we began to see miracles take place!

I could go on and on about the amazing things I've seen God do. We really have to make sure we stay prayed up before we go out there, and before we get into our cars to go home. Demons will look for vessels to inhabit so it's important to be covered by the blood of Jesus!

The Lord also called me to sing out there on the streets. I have to admit I was a little intimidated at first because several people get offended when we mention the word Jesus. They'll threaten us and try to do everything they can to keep us from ministering to others. All these thoughts started running through my mind. Just the many spirits we deal with alone makes me understand why people fear street ministry. The first day I went out there I felt the Lord and His peace and it was so incredible, just the boldness that He has given me to do as He has called me to do.

I don't have the most powerful voice, but people are moved! I don't have any instruments,

no musical accompaniment, nothing to jazz up the sound. Just my voice a cappella and nothing else that I lift up to God. When I sing I feel such a strong presence like it's just me and the Lord! And I know He is pleased. It reminds me of the song The Heart of Worship. We have so much that we can bring and offer to the Lord. Even if you don't think you can sing or have the most beautiful voice. When you come before Him and your heart is pure and you give all that you have to Him in your praise, the Lord is honored by that offering you bring to Him.

Then the Lord showed me that a lot of times we focus our praise and worship on the sound that we hear. We don't think about what the Lord hears. And it's crazy because the Lord hears our hearts. He doesn't really focus on the sound that's coming out of our mouth. When He hears and feels what's coming out of our hearts, that's what pleases Him, and when our worship goes up to Him and we're giving it all to Him that is the most beautiful sound that can be heard and that's what our Father hears. It was really healing for me to know that my voice and my sound is

pleasing to the Lord and I'm just as important as that person that has spent their entire life learning music and how to sing. He revealed to me how important it is to bring heaven down to earth. To take people to a place where they can feel God's love overflow.

I was no longer worried about those who may threaten. I just focused on praising the Lord, and it being a sweet sound to the Lord's ear. God will bring the people your way that He wants you to touch and reach and He has proven that out there.

FOUR

Spiritual Warfare

When you are doing the Lord's work you will get attacked by the enemy so it's important to stay prayed up even before you leave your house. Everything is spiritual.

Just this past year in May of 2021 I got in the worst accident that I had ever been in my entire life. Me and my entire family, which is my husband and 2 kids, were out running errands. We were at a stop light when a vehicle that was speeding hit us head on. It became a 5 car collision and it was terrible! I was looking down at the time so I didn't see the car coming that hit us. I'm so thankful to God for that because I know from the way I react that if I had reacted, it could have caused more serious damage to my body. My kids walked out of that accident with just sore muscles and abrasions. My husband and I walked out of there with abrasions, a sore neck, and pain in the chest, shoulders and back. We were messed up for a while to where we could hardly do anything that first week. We had to go to physical therapy for a month, but I thank God that he still has a purpose for me and my entire family. With all the deaths that are going on He could have decided to take us out, but He still has purpose for us.

Even though the enemy tried to take my family out, took away my vehicle and tried to scare me and stop what I was doing, that did not stop me from ministering and continuing on with what the Lord had planned
.

I hope this encourages someone to not give up even though the enemy will attack. When you are doing work for the Lord you do become a threat. Keep enduring and the Lord will see

Spiritual Warfare

you through and bless you more than you can imagine.

The Lord has blessed the Jesus Is Lord Street Ministry Team tremendously. We've had several people who have given so generously to help us out. We had a couple donate a wagon to the team to help us carry our food, water, clothing and other necessities out there. We had some people donate clothes, etc. The one gift someone donated that truly blessed us is the baptism pool that we now have, and continue to use to baptize many who decide to give their lives to Christ.

We now preach at the park at a little stadium where people can sit down and enjoy worshiping with us. We give them water, coffee, food, tracts and pray for them individually. We also pray for the community, worship, allow others to give their testimonies, minister a word and sometimes we will baptize. People come to listen from all around. Families that are walking by with their children, the workers out there, the homeless, students that go to the college in that area and more all come to listen and take part.

FIVE

The Lord's Desire

*A*s Christians it is our job to tell others of the good news of Jesus Christ and that perfect work that He has done for us on the cross. Use your testimony of what the Lord has done in your life to build other people up. **And they overcame him by the blood of the Lamb, and by the word of their testimony; and they loved not their lives unto the death.** — Revelation 12:11.

The Lord is building you up for more. Allow Him to take you higher. Throughout my life the Lord has given me friends that were only for a season. The Lord has shown me that we may all change spiritually in life with friends, family, our brothers, sisters and leaders in Christ and even with our spouses. And I will talk about the struggles with each that I have experienced as I have grown deeper in my relationship with Christ. We need to continue pressing on towards God regardless of what others think of us. That is very very important! Some may say you are way out there but in 1 Peter 2:9 KJV the word of God reads, **But ye are a chosen generation, a royal priesthood, an holy nation, a peculiar people; that ye should shew forth the praises of him who hath called you out of darkness into his marvelous light.** Do not be conformed and get comfortable with what is going on in the world. If you are around friends who say that they are not going to live their life a certain way where they are asking "What would Jesus do in this situation?" Then you should ask yourself what God is revealing to you about who you are allowing into your circle. Some people are meant to continue forward and some are from older seasons. Sometimes the Lord needs to prune people out of your life to take you higher in Him. You will come out refined and more like Him. Hallelujah!

The Lord's Desire

With family that is on a different spiritual level it gets hard. The church you grew up in may have taught something different than the truth that God has revealed to you. The Lord may reveal to you certain spirits that are on family or around them that you don't want to tell them about because you are worried about looking crazy. You may even find out that the spirit of God isn't even in some of the churches that you visited. This is the point where you have to just lay all things at God's feet and allow Him to reveal to others what they don't see. The Holy Spirit reveals all. Prayer is so powerful and when we begin to intercede and stand in the gap for our family and loved ones, chains begin to break and generational curses begin to fall off and become void. Continue to pray over your family and the bloodline. Repent and renounce all evil off of their lives. We have to stay repentant and when it all comes down to it, allow God to be glorified through you and use you as His willing vessel. When you stand before the living God on that glorious day you want Him to be pleased. The rewards in heaven will be greater when you endure hardships as well.

With ministers and people with great titles the struggle can be that many come off controlling. You have to move at the level where God is calling you to be. Don't move any faster or any slower than God wants for you. It's important to make sure that you aren't changing for a person, but are changing because that is what God wants for your life. It's also so important to hear God's voice and allow the Lord to lead and guide you to the right people because there are so many people who are Christians that don't have that right relationship with God. Pray and ask the Lord for wise counsel concerning your leaders. We can't listen to the voice of every person and have to use the spirit of discernment. When we read the word and ask God to show us the truth He will reveal it to us. He will give us wisdom, knowledge and understanding. The Lord is not the author of confusion. Sometimes it is wise that if you are going through a period of confusion to not allow anyone to minister a word to you except for God. Taking time to find a quiet place each day to get away from noise and just spend time alone with God talking to Him is so important. Remember to keep God 1st place and He will be honored by that!

It can be a lot more difficult if you are on a different spiritual level than your spouse. The advice that a friend told me is that it is anticipated and expected that people grow in different ways in marriage over time for various reasons, including spiritual reasons. Like with everything, meet your spouse half way and try to see things from their point of view. You can still cater to their point of view while holding on to God. God won't go anywhere, but you may risk losing your spouse whether physically if they left or intimately if they distance themselves. Remember they married someone specific, if you change drastically, then you are no longer the person they married and they may disinvest, and God wouldn't want that. God is not going away so make your decisions with wisdom not alienating either, while you continue to pray for your spouse.

There is so much that I'm learning in life and that God continues to show me. The one thing that I have noticed is that as I am growing so much in Him. I am not always comfortable with the change in every season of my life because I'm walking in a new phase of life. Whether it's a comfortable season or not we should not sit and be complacent, but be open for change.

Let's make God happy and not worry about what others may say. Be instant in season and out of season for God! Allow the Lord to speak to you, listen and harken to His voice.

SIX

Go Deeper in Christ

When you go deeper with God He will take you to an awesome level that is unlike anything that you can imagine. He will take you higher in Him. He will start connecting you to the right people at the right time who have a word for you. He will show you what and who to get rid of out of your life. He will start opening up and expanding your visions and dreams. He will open your eyes up to see things in the spiritual realm that you were blinded by before. He will open up doors on your behalf and show you things that you weren't able to see before. There is so much that the Lord has to reveal. He is building you up for more. I am ready and excited for the Lord to reveal more in this season!

This life is a spiritual battle that we are facing daily and there are so many things to distract us everyday. The shopping, going on trips, planning birthday parties, making sure our kids are smarter than average, watching the latest box office hit, where we are going to eat... We have to stay in the spirit daily and remember that we are at war here on this earth. We are on this earth to win souls for Christ. People are out there that the enemy is trying to steal from God's kingdom. Our fight is for the lives and souls of others. Let's not let the enemy steal what does not belong to Him. If we make it a goal for us to tell someone about Christ daily we are doing a tremendous work for the Lord. Let's stay awake and not be asleep when Christ returns for us.

Regardless of where you are in life the Lord can use you. We all have unique gifts and talents that the Lord has given us. Listen for God's voice and be alert to where He has called you to be. There is so much work to be done out there and the Lord invites you to join Him in getting it done.

SEVEN

A Promised Crown

To anyone who thinks that they are only ordinary, remember that you are a masterpiece and child of the most high God! The Lord wants to use you just like you are. If you have accepted Him as your personal Lord and Savior, you have a promised crown waiting for you.

The Lord is coming back quickly. Take hold of your crown and don't let anyone take it away. It has already been bought and paid for so wear it proudly!

Blessed is the man that endureth temptation: for when he is tried, he shall receive the crown of life, which the Lord hath promised to them that love him. — James 1:12 KJV

The Promise Ring Crown

I have fought a good fight, I have finished my course, I have kept the faith: henceforth there is laid up for me a crown of righteousness, which the Lord, the righteous judge, shall give me at that day: and not to me only, but unto all them also that love his appearing. — 2 Timothy 4:7-8 KJV

Fear none of those things which thou shalt suffer: behold, the devil shall cast some of you into prison, that ye may be tried; and ye shall have tribulation ten days: be thou faithful unto death, and I will give thee a crown of life. — Revelation 2:10 KJV

Behold, I come quickly: hold that fast which thou hast, that no man take thy crown. Him that overcometh will I make a pillar in the temple of my God, and he shall go no more out: and I will write upon him the name of my God, and the name of the city of my God, which is new Jerusalem, which cometh down out of heaven from my God: and I will write upon him my new name. — Revelation 3:11-12 KJV

EIGHT

An Heir of God

Make a promise to the Lord today that you will keep Him 1st place in your life for the remainder of your time here on earth.

DON'T GIVE UP
STAY FOCUSED
GIVE GOD YOUR ALL
RENEW YOUR MIND
BE INSTANT IN SEASON
ALLOW GOD TO HAVE HIS WAY
PRESS ON TOWARDS THE GOAL
BE WATCHFUL AND PRAY
WALK IN THE SPIRIT

Let thy garments be always white; and let thy head lack no ointment. — Ecclesiastes 9:8 KJV

For I am jealous over you with godly jealousy: for I have espoused you to one husband, that I may present you as a chaste virgin to Christ. — 2 Corinthians 11:2 KJV

Thou hast a few names even in Sardis which have not defiled their garments; and they shall walk with me in white: for they are worthy. He that overcometh, the same shall be clothed in white raiment; and I will not blot out his name out of the book of life, but I will confess his name before my Father, and before his angels. — Revelation 3:4-5 KJV

Let us be glad and rejoice, and give honour to him: for the marriage of the Lamb is come, and his wife hath made herself ready. And to her was granted that she should be arrayed in fine linen, clean and white: for the fine linen is the righteousness of saints. — Revelation 19:7-8 KJV

Prayer of Salvation

Have you given your Life to Christ? Do you know where you will spend eternity? If you don't this is the time to ask yourself, "How have I spent living my life?" It is something to think about. One day we will all stand before God to give an account of our life. We are not promised tomorrow. Make sure you are covered by the blood of Jesus and have the Holy Spirit dwelling inside of you. If you would like to accept Jesus Christ into your heart as personal Lord and Savior please say this salvation prayer below. Remember, it's not the words of the prayer that save you, it's the repentance and faith in your heart that lay hold of salvation. The Lord knows your heart, so trust in Him and allow Him to seal you with the Holy Spirit today.

The Promise Ring Crown

Dear God I come to you in prayer admitting that I am a sinner. I ask you to forgive me of all of my sins. I confess with my mouth and believe in my heart that Jesus Is your Son, And that he died on the Cross at Calvary that I might live and have Eternal Life in the Kingdom of Heaven. Father, I believe that Jesus rose from the dead and I ask that you come into my life and dwell will me. I ask you to be my personal Lord and Savior. I repent of my Sins and choose to put you 1st place in my life for the rest of my time here on earth. I confess with my mouth that I am born again and cleansed by the blood of Jesus. In Jesus name, Amen.

If you have just prayed that prayer welcome into the family of God. Talk with a church leader about baptism and the next steps toward your faith and walk with Christ. Depend on God like never before and get to know Him through His word. Two books of the Bible that I would recommend is the Gospel of Mark and John. Remember to tell others about what the Lord has done for you. God bless you!

About the Author

Tiffany Anita McClure has been happily married to an amazing man for 12 years. They have an adorable 9 year old boy and 4 year old toddler girl. Tiffany's family and her Lord and Savior Jesus Christ are everything to her.

Tiffany Anita McClure got saved and baptized at the young age of 8 years old. She went through some rough times where she strayed away. Tiffany knew that something was missing and she rededicated her life later on. Jesus knows who are His and who recognize His voice. **My sheep hear my voice, and I know them, and they follow me. — John 1:27 KJV**

Tiffany Anita McClure grew up in South Carolina but currently resides in Georgia. When she is not working, she enjoys spreading the gospel in street ministry, singing, editing and recording video, spending time with her husband and beautiful babies among other family and friends, watching movies, shopping and eating (She is such a foodie)! Tiffany loves swinging on her porch swing, spring flowers, long summer days and warm nights, fall leaves and snow days. Most of all, she loves God and her family! Loving life!

Please visit Tiffany on her YouTube channel:
Time with Tiffi

Her website is:
www.tiffanyanitamcclure.bigcartel.com

About the Author

www.ingramcontent.com/pod-product-compliance
Lightning Source LLC
Chambersburg PA
CBHW072040080526
44578CB00007B/542